Published by: Destinée Media
www.destineemedia.com

Chief Editor: Peco Gaskovski
Cover design by Ben Stone
Cover and interior by Ben Stone
Formatting by Ben Stone

ISBN 978-1-938367-74-8

Table of Contents

Comprehensive Spirituality

By Ellis Potter

What is spiritual?

Once, at an Evangelical leadership conference in Poland, I asked
people to tell me what they mean when they say "spiritual".
Several responses came in rapidly:

Supernatural

Invisible

Something Inside Me

Not Physical

Transcendent

I told people that I found these answers very interesting, as they
had just rejected the Incarnation and Resurrection of Christ as
unspiritual. The Bible is emphatic that these events were physical.
Without Christmas and Easter, Christianity is not what the
Bible says it is.

The purpose of this book is to explore and clarify what spiritual
means—a subject of much confusion. An understanding of
spiritual as supernatural is quite common among both religious
and non-religious people. As an equation, this understanding can
be expressed as:

spiritual = supernatural

I don't agree with this equation, and would put a line through the
equal sign, like this:

spiritual ≠ supernatural

As just mentioned, two central events of Christianity are the

Incarnation and Resurrection of Jesus Christ. When the Bible talks about these events, it emphasizes that they are physical, visible, touchable, and historical.

Perhaps a better equation for understanding spirituality, and the one that will be explored in this book, is the following:

spiritual = totally real

If spiritual equals totally real, then it is important to have some understanding of what reality is. Intelligent and alert students ask about this. Reality is who God is, what He does, and what He wants. This includes you, of course, because God wants you to exist and He made you. It includes the whole natural creation as God intends it to be. It includes the supernatural dimensions, forces, and creatures.

Distortions of who God is, what He does, and what He wants, are not real. They are not permanent but temporary. Eternity is permanent; time is temporary. Time is not evil, but it will end. Sickness, suffering and death, as well as pride, envy and hatred are not eternally real; they too will end. An exception is the suffering of Christ, which happened both in eternity as well as time, and therefore is real.

Within time, we suffer from sickness and death and other things, but they are not part of who God is, what He does, and what He wants. What is not real causes suffering. A paranoid person suffers terribly from delusions that are not real. The suffering does not make the delusions real. The unreal distortions that we experience are things that God wants to save us from and eliminate.

Sin is inventing unreality, and trying to live in it. The reality of God includes, as a major ingredient, humility. If I live in pride and being self-centered, then that is unreal, and I cannot live in that false, invented reality, because there is nothing to sustain it. I have to live in God's reality, of who He is, what He does, and what He wants. If I go outside of that, I will die. It's like the bird choosing not to migrate. It will die. That is why the Bible says *the wages of sin is death.*

Sin is not any particular activity, although particular activities participate in sin. Sin is basically going outside the parameters of reality, rebelling against the very rich reality in which we can have infinitely creative and beautiful lives, and inventing our own reality. That is what sin is, and it happens in big ways and in little ways, in our thoughts and in our speech, and in our actions.

Human beings throughout history have had a natural tendency to worship their imagination, and the imaginations of each other, and to consider them to be real—and sometimes more real than the actual reality. When we do that, it's not possible to live as an individual, as a community, or as a society, because there is no foundation to sustain or support that invented reality.

The way forward is to go back to the Bible, not in a religious sense of memorizing and reciting prescribed texts, or having certain emotional reactions to it, or looking inside ourselves to interpret it, but to read the text and ask, *What is the reality that the Bible describes in basic terms?*

Once we start to see the parameters of that reality, we can start to try and live in that reality, and to invite other people to live in it. For people, who are all sinners, accepting this invitation can produce a great transformation, because it involves going from a largely false reality and false identity to a true one. This change is described in the Bible as being *born again.* To be born again means being remade by the power of the sacrifice of Jesus Christ, and to live in the actual and true reality forever.

The creation is real, but the distortions of the creation that have come through sin are not real. Sin is any distortion, rebellion, departure or addition to reality. God is other-centered and He made people in His image to be other-centered. When we are self-centered and egotistical, that is unreal, and we have suffered terribly from that distortion.

To be spiritual is to be real as we should be, according to God's character and intention. To be spiritual means to belong to God and to fit into His reality. To be unspiritual is to shrink, expand, or distort God's reality. In 1 Corinthians 13, Paul writes about love. Here is another equation:

God is love

Paul tells us that no matter what we do or achieve or make, if we don't have love, we are like a gong in the wind—the sound dissipates and is gone. It is unreal. In the Old Testament, in the Psalms, we read that the person who bases his life on unreality will disappear like a dream upon waking.

Let's consider human spirituality as a series of triangles.

Creativity

The background of the first triangle is God. If we want to know what "spiritual" means in the biblical understanding of it, we need to begin with the Bible, which says "God is Spirit". This statement is the same as the statement "God is love", "God is light", or "God is truth". It means that everything about God is spirit, that there is no part of God that is not spirit or spiritual. So, in order to understand what spiritual means, we need to find out from the Bible who God is and what He is like, and then we will begin to get an understanding of what spiritual means in the biblical sense.

The first thing we learn about God in Genesis is that He creates and He speaks. He creates in an original sense of calling something into being that was not there before, such as time, space, and matter. God created the building blocks or foundation of the world, and He created the particular things in it; land, sea, plants, animals, as well as relationships of increasing complexity as the days of creation unfold. Then He said, *Let us create man (people) in Our image.* In creating people in His image, He therefore created them to be creative, because He is creative. If God had not done so, people would not be in His image, and would be incomplete.

The creativity of people is not an original creativity that calls time, space and matter into being, but rather continues the process of God's creativity. That process, according to the Genesis account, is the dividing of reality into parts to create relationships and dynamism. Reality was not meant to be static, undifferentiated matter, but seas and land, animals and plants, with contrasts, relationships, and energetic change. Reality is divided into parts, not for the purpose of exclusion or creating competition, but to make complementary relationships. When God made people, He made them to continue that process in a way that the other parts of creation do not.

People were placed on Earth, initially in the Garden, in order to tend and increase the complexity of the relationships that God had already made. One of the first things we see is that God had Adam name the animals. He divided the animals into a taxonomy, or categories, to make relationships between the animals. When he named them, applying labels to them, that's what they were. Naming them changed the reality. Naming them changed the relationships. The act of naming is a powerful function. A great art critic once wrote that the artist says *This is like that,* and everyone else says *It is! I never noticed that before!*

It is the function of the artist to help people see relationships, and similarly, it was the function of Adam to perceive, describe, and organize the relationships in the creation. The other animals did not have this job. It was only the human beings. Showing relationships through words, image, music, dance, clothing design, architecture, and so on, is not optional for the human being. Without artistic creativity, humans are not in the image of God or spiritual, because God is creative and shows relationships. It is essential to practice this kind of creativity in order to be spiritual.

Creativity can be dangerous. It can go wrong, and be wrongly used for pride, ego, conflict, domination, and evil, but it cannot safely be eliminated. We cannot make ourselves pure and spiritual by becoming uncreative. We need to accept that God has made us to be creative, and we must not refuse to be creative.

Creativity is not restricted to painting and music and other activities we might think of as "artistic". In the most basic sense, creativity involves identifying and organizing relationships, and making new relationships. For instance, wheat naturally grows along the side of streams mixed with other plants. The human being, being creative, says, *Wheat, you will grow in this field, alone.* That is not natural. That is artificial. The human being is called to be artificial. That is what art means. In other words, there's a division between art and nature. If something is natural, it's what God does, and it's right, true, and beautiful, but it isn't art. Art is artificial. It's made by the arm of man. A wheat field is not made by God, it is made by the human being, with imagination, research, experimentation, and physical strength. As a result, there is civilization; people can be stabilized, and don't need to be hunters and gatherers. But it's also art, in that it creates and organizes relationships within what God has made. Cooking, hospitality, interior decorating, conversation, child-rearing, education—all of these, like wheat fields, are creative, because they involve recognizing and organizing relationships.

Creativity is one of the things that makes human beings unique. It is part of God's perfect design and plan. If we say, *No, creativity is too complex and dangerous, and we are going to make our lives pure by eliminating creativity,* then we are disobedient and rebellious. An example of this disobedience would be a person with a talent for writing, who chooses to restrain himself from writing out of fear it is prideful or too powerful and might manipulate people— as if, by living a smaller and narrower life, he can keep his life clean and pure. Jesus said *I have come that you would have life, and have it more abundantly.* He didn't say *I have come that you would have life and have it tidily.* Life is a mess, and Jesus knows that. It's abundant and complex. We don't walk by control and sight, we walk by faith. In situations that are too complex for us to comprehend or control, we need to trust God to keep us safe. We have a natural tendency to reduce and control life, whereas the spiritual tendency is to obey God and to accept the complexity and the responsibility of creativity.

However, there is another and opposite danger. We may try to become God through our creativity. Keeping with the example of writing, the writer may create a fictional world which promotes concepts of human life, relationships, and values in order to replace what God has made. We see this tendency in many movies as well. A quite different example would involve agriculture. We have the power and the mandate to reshape plant life artificially, and to grow things in ways that they would not naturally grow. But this power can be misused to deforest a mountain range, or to cause erosion resulting in dustbowls; in this way, we irresponsibly and stupidly turn nature into our enemy by trying to control it.

The power that God has given us to be creative is not safe. We have to be careful and look as widely and deeply as we can into a situation, in order to be creative in a right way, within the posture of a creature rather than the posture of God. We need to function in a *creaturely* way. We create in the face of God, who has shown us some basic patterns, and we shouldn't replace those basic patterns with our own imaginations. We need to function within those patterns. But it's very complicated; I don't think we can see a way to draw a line, and to say "we figured it out, now we know"—because we don't know. Things change, and we always have to stay awake. We need to think, and talk and pray for wisdom, and that God will restrain us.

It is a natural tendency to want to draw a line to protect us, but it won't work. We will never find the right line, the exact boundary where we can say *this kind of creativity is safe,* and this kind of creativity is unsafe, because God has not designed us to live by law and fact only, but by faith, grace, and relationships, which are dynamic. Lines are static. It's not how God has created us to be.

God is not static. God is both unchanging and changing. We cannot comprehend the nature of God because we are creatures. In order to understand God, we would have to get behind Him and look over His shoulder to see the whole picture. But we can't see the whole picture. We have to walk by faith, not by knowledge or comprehension, though we very strongly want to understand and control. We want to simplify things so that life is easier, and so that "we get it". But the Bible shows us that we don't get it. We constantly need God to guide us, protect us, and restrain us. We need God to keep us safe through the impossible complexity of creativity.

The Second Triangle:

Rationality

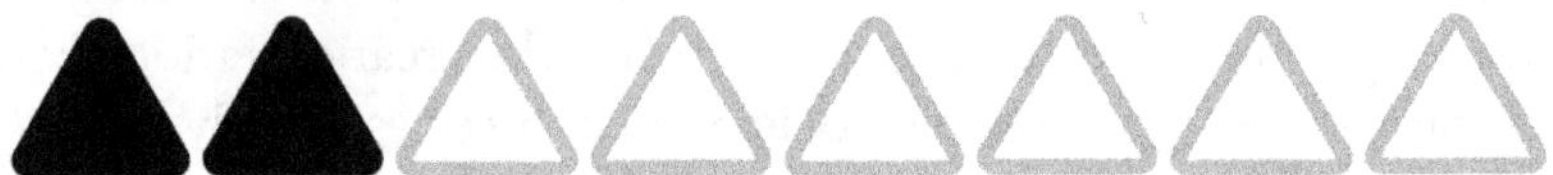

The second triangle is rationality. Rational means perceiving reality in relationships, or ratios. It means perceiving that parts of reality are bigger or smaller, faster or slower, brighter or duller, harder or softer. It means seeing a variety of qualities, such as size, intensity, shape, function, and so on, and to see how these different parts of reality relate to each other. The creation account in Genesis shows us specifically, and in detail, that God is rational. The whole process day by day, is creating and observing relationships, and calling them "good". The relationship of the land to the sea—it is *good*. The relationships among plants and animals and water creatures—they are *good*. The creative process is one of creating relationships of greater and greater detail, and rationality means seeing and understanding these relationships.

When God created creatures in His own image, they were rational. They were not rational as creators of the universe, but as unique creatures, different from the other parts of the creation. The non-human creatures do not perceive the creation rationally in the same way that people do. People do it very similarly to the way God does it.

Rationality and creativity overlap in some ways, but rationality is more a process of identifying and seeing with greater clarity what is already there; to be creative is to do something with those relationships, especially by making new relationships. Rationality is observing plants grow, and coming to an understanding of how they grow, whereas creativity is altering the way that they grow, for example by isolating plants in certain fields. Rationality gives us information about things, and therefore is essential; but creativity is also essential, because we do things with what we learn.

To be spiritual is to be the way God made us to be, and to be like God. Rationality is an essential part of spirituality, though it isn't problem-free. We can misuse our rationality. We can rationalize things in a legalistic or mechanical way. We can justify unjust behavior by certain forms of reasoning. We can sin in deadly ways with our logic. That makes people want to be safe, and therefore many people believe and practice becoming less rational. They try to live only by faith, only trusting impulses and instincts, or following their heart, and avoiding thinking things through and making rational decisions, because it feels to them more pure and simple to live only by faith. The goodness of that feeling is identified as a godly feeling, a spiritual feeling, whereas actually it is not. It is more like the feeling of a drug trip. It feels good, and so they think it must be true, when in fact other criteria are needed to evaluate goodness or non-goodness.

To evaluate in terms of how *I feel* is humanistic. It's not Christian. It means *I am God.* My feelings, my reactions, tell me what is good and what is evil. I don't trust God to tell me. I don't trust God's word, which is complicated; I trust my simple feelings, and gut-level ways of relating to the world around me. I protect those ways by keeping them simple and refusing to accept the complications of being rational. People sometimes say, *My mind is made up and don't confuse me with the facts. I'm a simple person of faith. I just trust and obey*—whereas they are neither trusting nor obeying, because they are eliminating the rationality that God intended to be part of their spirituality.

Of course our rationality is limited, for several reasons. First, we are creatures rather than the Creator, which means we never see and understand everything—far from it. Second, our rationality is limited by sin, by the distortions of our minds; and third, by being the victims of the sins of other people, whether our parents, ancestors, or those in our culture. Rationality is never perfect, and ideally it functions in complementarity with the other aspects of our spirituality. If we isolate rationality and expect it to give us life, we'll get death.

Rationality can also be distorted by history and culture. History and culture can swing like a pendulum toward different extremes.

Consider objectivity and subjectivity. The Enlightenment and the scientific revolution made a strong swing toward objectivity and the idea that *truth equals fact*. This swing resulted in various benefits in terms of scientific discoveries, discoveries which I'm actually quite thankful for. But it wasn't a whole picture. One of the things I'm thankful to postmodernism for is that it has restored subjectivity to truth, so that truth is not only objective or factual, but also includes individual and personal points of view. The problem with postmodernism is that, in restoring subjectivity to truth, it has to some extent eliminated objectivity. The one extreme is not better than the other, it's just different. What we need is a complementary balance of fullness and wholeness of objectivity and subjectivity.

How do we get to that balance? We get to it through prayer and trust. We get to it through the work of the Holy Spirit in our lives, transforming us and giving us the mind of Christ, rather than the mind of death. In this way, we can make progress in the direction of balance, although that process never finishes. No one can become perfectly balanced until the Lord appears and makes everything new. Until then, we remain in a situation that is imperfect. Sometimes people try to make things perfect, but perfectionism is a deadly disease—and yet, it is quite understandable, because God made us to be perfect. The longing for perfection is put in us by God; but to claim that perfection can exist through our own efforts, or to fear our lives have no meaning and no value because we haven't arrived at perfection, does not come from God.

Rationality cannot properly operate in isolation. Just as it must be balanced in terms of objectivity and subjectivity, it must be balanced with other areas of spirituality. We'll never get the balance right in a fallen world, though we will one day, in a redeemed world—and when it is right, it won't be right in a static, frozen sense, but in an active and dynamic eternity.

The Third Triangle:

Morality

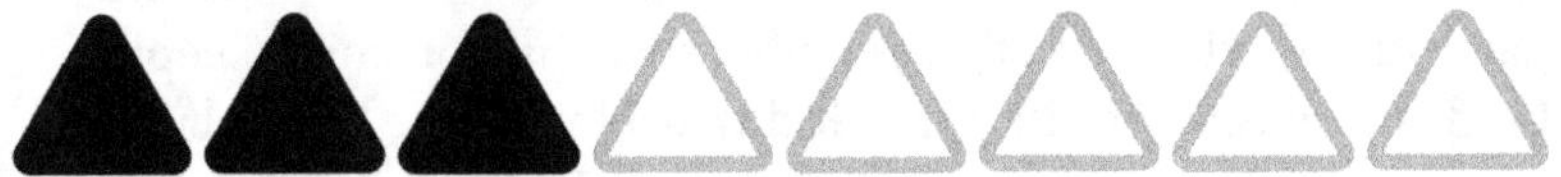

The third triangle is morality. Moral means being aware of what should be and what should not be. God is moral, as the Bible describes Him. He is aware that He should keep His promises, and not to be unfaithful or fickle. That should comes from Himself. No one created God. There is no uncle standing behind Him saying, *Now you be a promise-keeping God!* He is self-begotten. When Moses met God at the burning bush, Moses asked, *Who are you? What is your name?* God said, *I am that I am.* God is self-purposed, the cause of Himself. From our creaturely point of view that's unimaginable. How can there be a causeless cause? As far as we can see, everything that happens is caused by something else. And yet, God is the sole exception. He is the causeless cause. He is the final reality; and He is the beginning of everything.

God is aware of Himself as a causeless cause, and He is aware of His own nature. He isn't a cosmic gas cloud of love. He is a particular God—a creative, relating, speaking, promise-keeping God. There is a definition to God that He has for Himself and which He tells us about—*This is the way I am.* He knows that He *should* be a particular way. He should be a speaking God and *should not* remain silent. He *should* keep His promises, and He should not lie. He is completely consistent with what should be, and never does anything that He should not. He is faithful to Himself, and to His creation.

When God made human beings in His image, He also made them to be aware of should and should not. He gave them a specific example of that by putting the tree of the knowledge of good and evil in the garden, and telling them, *You should not eat from that tree.* The tree was a real tree, though it is also symbolic. The tree represents being independent and knowing good and evil for oneself, rather than receiving the knowledge of good and evil from God. If I choose to know good and evil from within myself, instead of receiving that knowledge from God, it means that I am God. I describe reality. I am the source of knowledge about good and evil. This knowledge comes from myself.

This belief produces death. It is death because it alienates me from my Creator. It also alienates me from other human beings who likewise have a sense of the knowledge of good and evil coming from themselves, although it's different from mine. So who is right? The differences are so great it doesn't work to say everybody is right, because that would mean there is no wrong. Of course some people like to think there is no wrong. But I've never met anyone who doesn't complain. I've never met anyone who hasn't said, *That's not right.*

But the idea that there is no wrong is strong in our world. You hear people say, *Everything is right,* or *Everything is okay.* Or they say, *There is no right or wrong. We are all on a journey. We don't know where we're going, but we don't need to know, and it's not getting there that's the point, the point is the journey itself.* If we really believed that, we could never logically complain about anything. Instead, we find ourselves compelled to complain, because things are wrong, objectively and subjectively. Everybody experiences things being in some way wrong—wrong in the world around them, and wrong in themselves.

The belief that everything is right, and that we are okay as we are, is an especially attractive idea. It reflects our natural tendency to want to be rich in spirit. But this is not what the Bible teaches. In the Sermon on the Mount, in which the King, Jesus, gives the manifesto of the Kingdom, the first point is poverty of spirit. Poverty of spirit means *I know that I need God.* To have richness of spirit is to know that *I am good in myself, and self-sufficient. I have a right to be affirmed. I don't need to be forgiven, I need to be empowered. I need society to give me what it owes me. I am entitled.*

I am okay in myself. Poverty of spirit is to realize I'm not fine, I'm not okay. I need to be forgiven. I need to be changed. I need to be healed. That is the first point of the Kingdom of heaven: If you don't have poverty of spirit, you will never have any relationship to the Kingdom of heaven.

Trusting in the message of Jesus is not purely a matter of faith. If I observe my life honestly, then what I observe is a mess. I see my wretchedness. I experience my alienation from others. The Bible encourages me to see that my life is a mess not because I was *made* a mess, but because I have *chosen* to mess myself up. Sometimes it can be hard to admit these things. Our natural pride can get in the way of seeing ourselves clearly. We can also be made blind by evil forces that want to consume us. The Bible teaches that the devil prowls around like a lion seeking whom he may devour. The devil speaks to people and encourages them with deadly thought forms and processes, empowering them for death. The combination of these two forces, our pride and an evil agency, can prevent us from recognizing the fundamental importance of poverty of spirit. They can prevent us from knowing that we need God.

Although the idea that *I am okay* is popular nowadays, the Bible is clear that people have believed this for all of history. Evil is very powerful, and people both get sucked up into it, and choose it, because it seems attractive. Once they have chosen it, it can become habit-forming; then people build a fortress around what is wrong and call it right. We defend our pride. We defend ourselves by saying, *No, I'm fine, this is the right way to go.* That's a real trap, and people need to be delivered. They need to be broken free of their enslavement to death. All of us are caught in this trap in one way or another, and all of us need to be set free.

Religious people, including Christians, often want very clear moral lines. It's true that some lines are drawn for us by God, and those should be accepted. A difficulty with those lines is that people exaggerate them, or minimalize them, or in some way distort the lines. Basically, the line that God has given us is the line between being self-centered and being other-centered. If we concentrate on ourselves getting and being served, and being affirmed in who we are in isolation, then we're moving in the wrong direction. If we think in terms of others, meaning God and other people, and how we contribute to and serve them, then we're moving in the right direction. So, it's probably better in some ways to think of a *direction* rather than a *line*. A moral line is not wrong, but a line is not enough. For instance, the Bible is clear that adultery is wrong. It's a line and we should not cross it. But when Jesus speaks about adultery, He speaks about adultery of the mind and the will, not just physical sex. He is speaking more in the sense of *what direction are you moving*. So if you refrain from having physical sex with someone that is not your spouse, you can still move in the direction of death through imagination, longing, obsession, and pornography. You can't just look at moral situations narrowly and think, *I haven't crossed the line, so I'm okay.*

God is the same God, with the same moral characteristics, throughout the Bible, both in the Old and New Testaments. That means God is morally consistent. Of course you will encounter people who claim that God is morally *inconsistent*, though they tend to hold this position as a matter of faith. It's also an excuse. If they can believe that God is wrong, then they're free. They can say, *I don't owe anything to God. There is no Creator. I just appeared evolutionarily like a mushroom out of the mold. I can be my own God.* That's a very strong impulse in the fallen world. It's another example of being rich in spirit.

When people approach me about the supposed inconsistency of God, I generally ask them, *What are the examples that you have in mind?* In my experience most people don't have any clear examples. They tend to offer more vague ideas like, *Isn't it true that the God of the Old Testament is legalistic, whereas the God of the*

New Testament is loving? But if you examine the Bible carefully and comprehensively, which most people don't, you find out that this claim of two Gods, one loving and one legalistic, is not true. It's the same God in both the Old and New Testament. So my advice is, if the question of God's consistency has any importance to you, then look into it. Investigate it thoroughly.

Along with carefully examining the Bible in order to understand God's consistency, I encourage people to carefully examine themselves. Sometimes people say, *Why doesn't God do something about evil, if He is all-powerful and all good?* My response to that is, *If God would do something about evil, what would He do about you?* This question can be a useful question. It's one of the most important questions that people wondering about God's moral character can ask themselves. If you are honest with this question, and honest in your investigation of the Bible, you will come up with answers that may surprise you. However, just because the question is useful doesn't mean that people will pay any attention to it. People are often like Teflon to these kinds of questions. In the New Testament, Jesus Himself, God incarnate, asked people questions, and they just slid off them like non-stick surfaces. God Himself was speaking to them face-to-face and it didn't help! Their pride was so strong that they had committed themselves to not considering any possibility other than what they believed. That was two thousand years ago. People are in the same situation now.

Pride can be so powerful and alluring that it can make it hard to see why we need poverty of spirit. When we have poverty of spirit, we accept ourselves as God has made us to be. We also accept God's opinion, which is much more positive than our own opinion—because God's opinion of us is that we are *worth* dying for. That is shocking. That is part of the scandal of the Gospel. God says *I made you, I love you. You are a wonderful creature, and you are lost. You are worth dying for. I want you to be with me so much that I'm going to die in order to have your company.* You can't

have a higher opinion than that. You can't get more positive than
that. The negative side is that you have to die. You have to die to
your ego, your pride, your self-centeredness, your desire to invent
yourself.

Dying like this is no easy thing. It can be painful and frightening.
The positive is that you get a much greater life. You die to your
deadly self, but you live in Christ. The positive far outweighs the
negative, although the negative is not negligible. The prospect
of dying can be excruciating. It can seem like open-heart
surgery without anesthetic. I'm sympathetic to this fear, but as a
Christian and a pastor I'm constantly encouraging people: Trust
God. Endure the pain. Endure the shock. Die to your deadly self
so that you can live in Christ. Choosing life may be hard, but it's
shocking that people don't want life. It's shocking, yet common
and understandable given all the pressures, temptations, and
natural proclivities of human existence.

Emotions

According to the Bible's description of God, He has emotions. He desires that people would live and not die. He desires that people would be well. He desires that people would be with Him and enjoy Him, and that He would enjoy them. He is angry when that doesn't happen—when people turn away from Him and destroy themselves or destroy each other.

We don't understand the emotions of God particularly well, but the Bible clearly says that they're there. Therefore, when God made creatures in His image, He made them to be emotional. We see this in the creation account. Adam was functioning as a human, but alone, which God said was *not good*, because the image of God is *them*, not *him* or *her*. Adam was just *him*, not them. Something essential was missing. When God made Eve, Adam was full of emotion and sang a kind of song in parallel Hebrew poetry. He was excited. Emotions were a part of who he was. They were present from the beginning.

We can make two mistakes when it comes to emotions. One is that, as we realize emotions are not stable and not trustworthy, we may try to avoid our emotions and make our spirituality only rational. We may try to simplify things and reduce our emotions. But to do so is wrong and destructive, because God made us to have emotions and to experience them.

The other mistake is to understand spirituality as only emotional. People may try to look for ways to induce emotional experiences, for example through contact with people, or by listening to certain kinds of music, or viewing certain kinds of art, or speaking in particular ways. People identify their private emotions, as well as public emotions they share, as spiritual, and end up discounting rationality or other aspects of spirituality. They feel safe and right with God, because they repeatedly have certain types of emotions they identify as spiritual. This tendency is a serious problem and a reduction of what spiritual means.

Both our emotional and rational sides are essential, but neither is entirely trustworthy. Still, people will tend to emphasize one or the other, and in doing so try to limit or eliminate the other. Rationality and emotions need to work together. Rationality without emotions isn't life. It's a computer. Emotions without rationality is also a problem, a problem of a different kind, though equally distorting.

In favoring emotions, people often gravitate toward certain types of emotion in defining spirituality. Emotions of happiness are often favored over emotions of fear or shame, although the Bible teaches us that fear and shame are part of what we should experience in a fallen world. We don't like those emotions, of course, and so it's the emotions that we prefer, the ones we identify as pleasant and pleasurable, that we tend to identify as spiritual.

I believe there is an emotion which, for lack of a better term, I would call hugeness. Think of what it feels like to be in an electrical storm, amid all the wind, lightning, and thunder. A feeling can arise in this situation which isn't fear, isn't joy, or anything like that, but *hugeness*—and people often identify *that* with spirituality. But I'd actually identify that feeling with the mob-like emotions of radical groups. Honestly, I myself have experienced that emotion in gatherings of thousands of Christians all singing together—a rush of the emotion of hugeness, which I really enjoy. I get exactly the same feeling when I listen to Beethoven, who wasn't particularly religious.

Some people think the feeling of hugeness or similar feelings, when they occur in a church, is the feeling of the Holy Spirit in them. But I doubt that the work of the Holy Spirit in our lives is principally experienced emotionally. I wouldn't eliminate emotion from the work of the Holy Spirit, but I wouldn't put the emphasis on it, because emotions can be counterfeited. Other workings of the Holy Spirit in our lives, like the fruit of the Spirit, are much more difficult to counterfeit. For instance, patience, kindness, goodness, and faithfulness are hard to fake. But emotions can be faked or stirred up fairly easily. You might even become less spiritual as your preferred emotions *increase.* I would put the emphasis on actual changes in our lives and attitudes when considering whether the Holy Spirit is working in us, rather than on the emotions we feel.

Sometimes people don't want to think carefully about their feelings. They may experience their feelings in a vague or fleeting way, and want to keep it that way. Then I would ask, *Would you also like to not know what food is poison and what food is nutritious?*

Some people seek out the experience, or feeling, of *oneness* with everything. They may find this experience through certain drugs, such as psychedelics, through certain forms of meditative practice, and sometimes through monist religions, such as Buddhism or Hinduism. But the experience of oneness is death. What does that mean? Consider that the beginning of reality is the Trinity, which is both one and many, both unified and diversified. When the Bible speaks of evil, it speaks of the devil, Satan, the accuser, who is only unified, with no diversity. There are no relationships within evil. It's like a black hole. Black holes are described as singularities, which is significant. The singularity is death; life as we know it cannot function in a singularity.

Some people claim that experiences of oneness can increase our feelings of peace and our compassion for others. I believe these people are sincere in their claims, but sincerity is not a criterion for truth. The devil is an angel of light, and attractive. The idea of oneness is attractive, but it is death. Of course death, in this sense, gives at least temporary benefit. It feels good. If we didn't enjoy sin, we'd never do it. The power of sin is its attractiveness. To properly assess experiences such as oneness, we always need to back up and remember a vital theological question: What is reality like? That is, what is *God* like? What does the Bible tell us? The Bible is quite clear that God is diverse. Jesus says *The Father and I are one.* There is a unity. But He also says, *I can only teach you what the Father teaches me. I don't know when the end of history will occur, only the Father knows.* So there is a difference between Jesus and the Father. When Jesus prays to the Father, He's not talking to Himself. He's talking to someone else. An extreme emphasis on unity—as in the idea of oneness—will not take diversity seriously at this fundamental level. As a result, it will distort and destroy reality.

If we want to avoid distorting reality in this way, then it would be useful to live within the circumference of reality. That can be difficult, as many people have lost any concept that there is a limit to reality. We have been taught that reality is how we feel about it. The meaning of a text is my response to the text. In dealing with such tendencies, I might ask people, *How are you feeling about gravity today? Do you feel that gravity pulls toward the Earth or pushes away from it—and let me respect how you feel.* Of course it doesn't matter at all how a person feels about gravity. It's a given. God has given us gravity, and although we may feel a variety of ways about it, those feelings don't change the reality. If we follow our feelings, it can be dangerous, especially if we feel very strongly that we can fly. So, it's important to realize the limits of the reality of our feelings. Not that they're not real, and not that we don't have to deal with them, and not that they aren't powerful and a part of who we are. But there is a limit on the power of feelings to create reality, and we need to respect that limit.

Within Eastern worldviews, the word *compassion*—rather than love—is often used in connection with oneness, and rightly so. Love is a face-to-face relationship. Love is exclusion and embrace. I realize you are different, you are other, you are there, and therefore I can embrace you. But if I experience unity with you, I cannot embrace you. I just hug myself. Compassion is an emotion and an activity that supports and draws people into an experience of unity. Love, although it can be an emotion, is primarily a series of choices that encourages the other person to be who they are, as other. That is how the Bible describes reality as it actually is.

When people refer to the *peace* that comes with oneness, it's hard to know what this precisely means, although, beyond a feeling, it often seems to refer to a *lack of conflict.* But that isn't peace in the biblical sense. In the Bible, peace refers to *shalom,* which means *the provision of a platform and a framework in which to have conflicts.* So, the peace of Jacob with God was expressed in wrestling. Jacob wrestled *with* God, not *against* God; and he wrestled for truth and identity. He became Israel—*he who wrestles with God, struggles with God.* Peace is not the elimination of struggle, but a stable context in which we can have struggle, and grow in truth. The elimination of struggle, of conflict, is the elimination of life.

At a global level, an increasing belief in the feeling of oneness can make people more susceptible to control, politically, economically, religiously, and in other ways. It would probably lead to dictatorship.

The Fifth Triangle:

Language

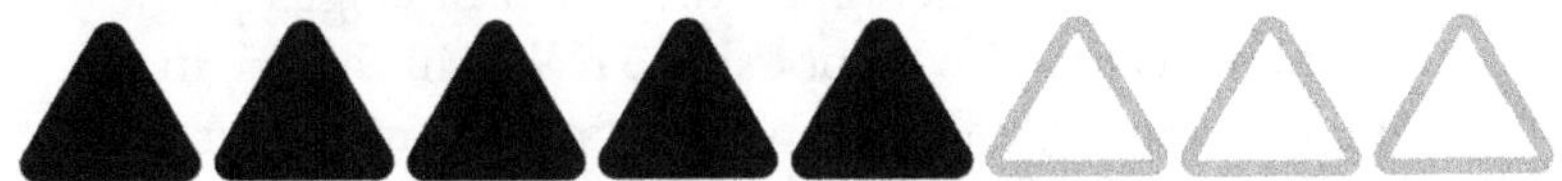

One of the first things we learn about God in the Bible is that He speaks. We learn that His speech creates reality. *Let there be light,* and there was light. *Let there be seas and land,* and there were seas and land. God spoke these things into reality. Then He made people in His image through words, and brought the animals to Adam to see what he would name them. He brought them, not to see if Adam would guess their names, or if he would remember the list of names that God had provided, but to see what he would name them out of his own imagination, out of his own formulation and creativity. Whatever Adam called the animals, that is what they were. As we saw, the animals were changed by being named, by being put in a taxonomy. T.S. Eliot wrote in his *Four Quartets: ...the roses had the look of flowers that are looked at.* In other words, once they are looked at, the roses are different from the flowers that haven't been looked at. Similarly, animals that are named are different from animals that have not been named. The human being has the power of language, the power to shape reality. We do not shape reality in the original sense of God creating reality out of nothing, but in the sense of *reshaping* the reality, of continuing the organizational process of developing relationships through language. So language is essential to human nature.

In order to be spiritual, we cannot eliminate language. It has to be there, but like the other triangles, it's not safe. We can misuse language. We can lie, we can manipulate it, we can use it in the wrong way. But we cannot be spiritual *without* language.

We need to take language seriously, and also need to rejoice in it. If we don't take it seriously, we can't rejoice in it. We need to acknowledge the power of language, and to acknowledge our responsibility in using it carefully. We need to say what we mean and mean what we say. We must not pretend that language is unreal, or that it has no effect. We should not constantly say *whatever* at the end of every sentence, or qualify everything by saying *like,* instead of what it actually is. We must not minimize the reality of language, or the power that it actually has.

When we take language seriously, we rejoice in our capacity to use it for description, for commitment, for relationship, for encouragement and enabling. Language has an enlivening function. Taking it seriously means learning to express ourselves using a variety of words. It means being aware of clichés, proverbs, or cultural phrases and examining those to find out what they actually mean, and whether we really mean those things, or if we hide behind them. Do we speak in a committed way, or do we hide behind groupthink? These are the kinds of issues we need to consider in order to deepen and enrich our use of language.

Clichés are especially problematic. Their meaning can be distant, diffuse, and broad. People rely on them, but they're not a direct, committed communication. Clichés don't promote relationships. They promote a shallow kind of identity. We may identify with other people who use the same clichés, and feel that we have a relationship with them, or belong with them in some way, but that's hardly any relationship at all. But if I speak what I mean to say, even if another person disagrees with me, then that's in fact a closer relationship. We speak to each other about a subject, and we know we see it differently. That's much closer than mouthing the same cliché.

We also see an increasing use of images and icons to express ideas. Images can be effective in some ways, but reductionistic in others. For instance, an emoji will not fully or clearly express an idea, whereas if I formulate a sentence to give to someone, it will be more direct, responsible, and meaningful.

Some people may feel they are not good at language. They may struggle with this aspect of spirituality. We all struggle with one or several aspects of spirituality. That's part of reality. It wouldn't be wise to say, *This part of spirituality is a struggle, so I'm going to eliminate it or despise it, or pretend it has no importance.* That would be a huge mistake. Life is hard. We need to encourage each other in the struggle of life. If someone struggles with language, then we need to support them and help them see that they do have linguistic powers that haven't been developed yet, and help them to become excited about the possibilities. The same could be said for emotions, rationality, and all the other aspects of spirituality. This is what love means. It means to act and speak in ways that encourage the other person in who God wants them to be. God wants us to be rich and powerful in all these different parts of spirituality. Each person tends to be stronger in some parts and weaker in other parts. We have a natural tendency to strengthen what is strong, and to ignore what is weak. But we have a spiritual tendency to strengthen what is weak, without ignoring what is strong.

Unfortunately, people tend to consider what comes most naturally to them as spiritual. That's a profound confusion between the natural and the spiritual. A person who is more naturally rational than emotional will have a tendency to call rationality spiritual, and to consider emotions a kind of voodoo. Instead, we need to encourage each other in our spiritual tendency, which is to have a more equal complementarity of the different aspects of spirituality.

The Sixth Triangle:

Relationships

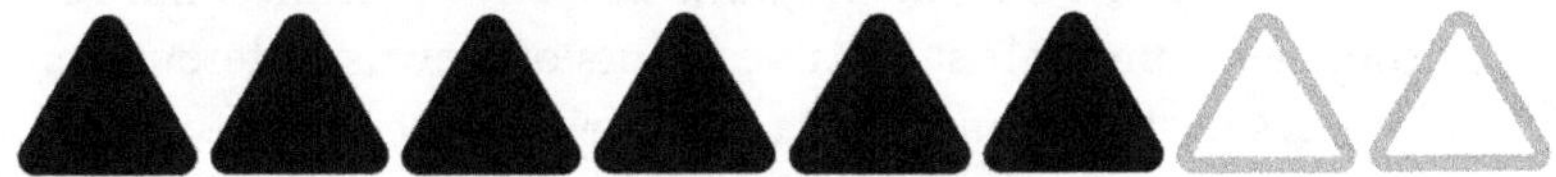

The Bible tells us that God is three Persons. They are not identical to each other, and in some ways they are opposite. For example, the Father commands and sends, and the Son obeys and goes. There is a dynamic variety of function and point of view in God, in the original reality. The Persons of God speak to each other, and have a hierarchical relationship with each other. Hierarchical relationships may be politically incorrect today, but Jesus was clear about the issue. He said that He could not teach anything He did not receive from the Father. He also said He does not know when history will end—only the Father does.

God objectively exists. The three persons of God each objectively exist. The persons of God seeing each other from their different points of view is subjectivity. The Father exists objectively and does not change. He is faithful to His character. The Son and Holy Spirit see the Father from different points of view, and so, although they are looking at the same objective Person, some of what they see from their subjective points of view is different. The Son sees perfectly, and the Holy Spirit also sees perfectly, so the differences in what they see are perfect.

One of the implications of this for the Christian life is that Christians should not be clones of each other, seeing everything in exactly the same way. The relationship between Christians should not be one of identity but complementarity, which means acknowledging, respecting, and treasuring the differences we have from each other. On the sixth day of creation, God said, *Let Us make man in Our image.* Then He created Adam. The other days, when He created the lands, the sea, the stars, the plants, the animals, He said, *It is good,* and even, *It is very good.* But, as mentioned earlier, when He created Adam He said, *It is not good.* What was not good is that Adam was alone. *It is not good that the man should be alone.* The reason it wasn't good is because God is not alone.

Here is a proverb I made up: *God alone is God, and God is not alone.* And yet, Adam, in the beginning, was alone. There was no other. He could relate to God, which is essential and beautiful, but *within* the creation there was no one for him to relate to. Adam was aware of himself, and aware of his environment, and had an effect on his environment in naming the animals. Most people would think Adam was personal, but he wasn't. To be personal requires relationships with other persons. To be personal is very different from identity—from "self-being". It is self-being in relationship with other self-beings. Adam didn't have that. He only had himself. God brought the animals to Adam to see what he would name them, and perhaps for Adam to discover that there was no parallel relationship for him with the animals.

Animals are different from human beings. So are plants. They function within the parameters of what God made with total faithfulness. For instance, many birds are made to migrate. They migrate every year without fail, often on the same day, or they die. Similarly, if you hike up the Alps and see a flower, you notice that ten meters higher you don't see that flower anymore. If the seeds from that flower drift a few meters too high or too low, they won't germinate, or they germinate and they die, because they, like other plants and animals, have a natural habitat and natural ways of functioning. If they go outside those parameters, they die, they can't exist. But the human being, who is made in God's image, changes the patterns. The human being is the pattern-breaker. The human being tends the garden, the human being begins with what God has made, and makes changes to it. It's like the example I gave about wheat. God made wheat, and then human beings made wheat to grow alone in fields. That's the kind of radical pattern change that the human being makes, and that the other animals (or plants) don't. But that doesn't make them personal. There has to be another self-aware person to relate to in order to be personal.

In a very real sense, one person is not in the image of God. Of course it's commonly thought that each person, each individual, is in the image of God, but the creation account shows that's not true. The Lord's Prayer also shows that's not true. The Lord's Prayer begins with *Our Father, not My Father.* It's not just me and God. Jesus has no concept that I would relate to God totally alone, that He would be my personal God and I would have a private relationship with Him. I have to relate to God in relationship with other people.

So Adam named the animals, and that was a powerful thing because it changed their nature. The act of naming made a difference in the world. But still the situation was not good because Adam was alone. There was no one to relate to in the Creation. So then God made Eve. Eve was similar to Adam in many respects; for instance, she was a pattern breaker like he was, had a subjective point of view, and so on, but she was also different from Adam. She wasn't a clone of Adam. There's a peculiar proverb in America: God made Adam and Eve, not Adam and Steve. Often this proverb is used against the gay community, but its real meaning speaks to something more fundamental. God didn't make human beings to look for sameness and to live within identity, but to live in relationships with differences. In the right relationship of Adam and Eve, there is a third—a child. That is how people are, basically, anywhere you look in history. There is a mother, father, and a baby. So, in a real sense, human beings come in sets of three, which shouldn't be surprising. God is three Persons, and His image is three Persons. People are Trinitarian. When God finished making Adam and Eve, and Adam and Eve were relating to each other, the Bible text says, *God made people in His image, in His image He made them.* So the image of God is not him or her, but them, in relationship.

The idea that people are Trinitarian has been individualized by some Christian teachings, in particular suggesting that each person is a tripartite organization of body, soul, and spirit. I believe this teaching is problematic, because it leaves out some things, like heart and mind. In that way, it's not comprehensive. But the bigger problem is it's all about the *self*, whereas Christianity is all about the *other*. It's about loving your neighbor as yourself, not about loving yourself. It's not about having a private relationship with God, but about having a relationship in a community—of family, friendship, neighborhood, church, business, nation, and other communities. So it seems to me more true to say that the human being does have a tripartite nature, but it isn't mind, body, and spirit; it's mother, father, and child. That is basic spirituality. So spirituality is not a private thing. You cannot really say, *I am spiritual.* You can only say, *We are spiritual.*

Today people want to believe they invent themselves. But the Bible teaches that we are given who we are. The fallen nature and sin of the world distorts what we are given, but fundamentally we are given who we are. When people insist on inventing themselves out of their longing, pain, or imagination, then they take away the possibility they are given anything. As a result, people can become very lonely. They can also put tremendous pressure on themselves, not only to invent themselves, but to sustain that invention. This pressure is especially hard on children and teenagers. I believe this is why we see increasing rates of suicide among youth. They cannot bear the pressure of being their own God. They cannot bear the pressure of creating themselves out of their own imagination.

The Seventh Triangle:

The Body

It is not possible to be spiritual without a physical body. Many people, if not most people, think of spiritual as transcendent and non-physical. But "spiritual" as described in the Bible is a fuller reality. God has created the physical world and He loves it. He has promised to restore it and sustain it forever. God's reality is not divided into spiritual and non-spiritual; it is all spiritual. Spiritual means a full and integrated reality; that which is partial and disconnected is unspiritual.

God's original intention was to have a physical incarnated body. God's original intention for us was also to have a physical body. The idea that "spiritual" does not include the physical is very old, and even the disciples of Jesus were troubled by it. Jesus's victory over death on the Cross resulted in His new spiritual resurrection body. When the disciples saw this body, they saw it through Platonic or Greek eyes. Palestine had been a Greek colony for three hundred years, since Alexander the Great, and the Greeks had control of the educational system. Jewish boys had absorbed Platonic thought, which includes the transcendental notion that "the idea" is more real than *the actual thing*—which the Old Testament doesn't teach. So, when the disciples saw Jesus appear to them in the locked room where they were staying, they thought they saw a ghost or a supernatural being. The first thing Jesus did was to tell them, *No, I am not a ghost, touch me. I am fully real.* He also asked them to give Him something to eat, and He ate it in their presence. In the new spiritual kingdom of God, touching is spiritual and eating is spiritual. The disciples were startled because Jesus did not come to them through the door or the window. He was able to appear to them, to simply materialize, because He was functioning both in the space-time dimensions, and the non-space-time dimensions, of reality. That is why He can teleport, appear and dematerialize. Jesus, in His resurrection body, functions in the whole reality. We function in, and are aware of, only part of the whole. When we become spiritual—fully spiritual one day in a redeemed world—we will be able to function in the whole reality, being totally real. That includes having a physical body.

In the Book of Luke, we read of Jesus meeting two disciples on their way to Emmaus. Emmaus is about four miles from Jerusalem, so it takes about two hours to walk the distance. The disciples were going home. Most paintings and etchings of Jesus meeting these two disciples shows two men. But it wasn't two men, it was Cleopas, who is named in the Biblical text, and Mrs. Cleopas—Mary Cleopas—who was present at the crucifixion. These two disciples are feeling down and disheartened at Jesus's recent death and all that has happened since then. Jesus said to them, *Why are you so sad?* They responded, in effect, *Are you a tourist? Don't you know what has been going on? The whole city is in an uproar. We thought the Messiah had come, but He was killed, although now there are some women who say they've seen Him alive, and we don't know what to do or think. Jesus replied, You are so slow of heart!*—and then He opened up the Scriptures and He showed them, from beginning to end on this long walk, why the Messiah must die and rise again to new life.

Then they reached Emmaus and they made Him come in and sit down to supper. In a Jewish home, then and now, at the beginning of the meal, the father picks up bread, and says, *We bless you, oh God, King of the universe, who gives us bread.* Then he breaks the bread and the meal begins. But when they sat down, Jesus grabbed the bread, which must have been a bit shocking. It was as if He was saying, *This is my house, I am the host here. This is my bread and I'm in charge.* Then He said the customary prayer, and He broke the bread and disappeared. At that point, the two disciples didn't say, *Weren't our hearts burning within us when He disappeared? No. And they didn't say, Weren't our hearts burning within us when He grabbed the bread?* What they said was,

Weren't our hearts burning within us when He talked with us on the road? So when Jesus was working with their heads, their hearts were burning, which shows us that the difference between the head and the heart is nothing. It all belongs together. Thinking, understanding, and perception are all part of spirituality. Spirituality is not only a transcendental or emotional reality. It's a rational and sensing reality as well.

In John 21: 4-13 we read about Jesus coming to the disciples at the Sea of Galilee. They had been fishing all night by torchlight, and He seems to say, *Hey guys, did you catch anything?* They replied, No, we didn't. He encouraged them to put in the net one more time. They replied that they had been doing it all night, but He insisted, so they did and landed an enormous catch. This was a miracle, but Jesus is the Creator of the universe and called the fish into the net. Then it dawned on the disciples who it was that was talking with them. They came to the shore and saw some surprising things. They found that Jesus had built a fire. He had been working, in other words. He had also baked bread, so He had been creative, and had broiled fish too. So we see that work is spiritual, and creativity is spiritual, because the resurrected glorified Christ did both. Then Jesus said, *Come, and have breakfast,* which shows us that practicing hospitality is also spiritual.

In the post-resurrection appearances above, Jesus is present physically, and emphatically so, walking, speaking, eating, working, which tells us that the physical body is also essential to spirituality. It tells us our physical body will be sustained by God forever. So, when we try to be spiritual, we should not try to neglect, or leave, or transcend the body. We should take the body seriously, not self-centeredly or narcissistically, but in the way God intended. We should thank God for it, and rejoice in it. Our physical body is not something that God is going to throw away.

It is something that He made, and will transform, along with transforming our minds and our hearts, and keep with Him, for us, forever.

The risen Jesus, as described in the Bible, is the final spiritual reality. There is no next step. Nothing else happens. This is it. Jesus is natural and supernatural. He is transcendent and immanent. When we belong to Him, *that* is the direction we are moving. Of course we don't know everything about what it will be like to be fully restored in this way, but we see indications of it in the resurrected Jesus, and we see it at the end of the Bible, in the wedding supper of the Lamb. That supper is not going to be the exchange of nutritious waves of ectoplasm between glowing light spheres. It's going to be broiled fish, and bread, and food of all kinds. People will enjoy it. They might even comment on the flavor. Of course there will be much more to that redeemed existence, because we'll be living in all the dimensions of reality, and we don't fully know what it will be like. What we can say, for certain, is that it will be a larger, richer, and more interesting life than the one we have now. Nothing will be taken away from what we have, except for our tears, weeping, pain, and mortality; but we will still have emotions and perceptions. There will not be any general reduction of life in order to have a spiritual life. Rather, things will be added to the life we already have. We cannot experience the fully redeemed existence now, but we can believe, accept, rejoice, and anticipate what is to come, through faith.

The Eighth Triangle:

The Supernatural

We have considered seven different aspects of spirituality, all of which are essential and work in a complementary relationship, forming a full spirituality. But one thing we have not talked about is the supernatural, which includes angels, demons, realms and powers, and prayer and the work of the Holy Spirit in our lives.

We are always in the presence of the supernatural, not only sometimes. To be spiritual requires the inclusion of the supernatural, and not living only in the created space-time continuum. We need to be in relationship with the *uncreated* reality, which is God. Sometimes I refer to the supernatural as the eighth triangle of spirituality, although I don't often emphasize it, because most Christians (and non-Christians) already know that spirituality involves the supernatural. The problem is, many people think that's all it involves, and that's why I emphasized the other seven triangles—to show that spirituality is more than the supernatural, although it's not less than the supernatural.

Prayer is a relationship with God. Some people want to learn about prayer techniques. Sometimes there can be techniques, but if prayer gets reduced to a technique, it is no longer what God intends it to be. Relationships are not techniques. Relationships are often the very opposite, even somewhat mysterious. The situation between ourselves and God is similar to a marriage. We are the bride of Christ. He is our husband, and we relate to Him in a variety of ways, one of which is prayer. People confuse prayer with meditation, transcendence, or emotional experiences; but fundamentally, prayer involves speech. It involves words. At the end of the prophecy of Hosea, he says, *Take words with you, and return to the Lord.* It may sound a little bit comical, like bring them in a bucket, but remember that the first thing we learn about God is that He speaks. His speech has effect, and He is faithful to His speech. The first thing we learn about people, as well, is they have speech. Adam named the animals, and his speech had effect. Words and speech are essential and basic to God and to God's image, human beings.

We can't overestimate the importance of words. We need to use them carefully. I've heard Christians use expressions like, *It's only words.* My response is, *What else is the Bible? What else in the Bible do we have, besides words?* There is nothing else. It's only words. Words are essential to human conversation and to prayer. When Jesus taught His disciples to pray, He didn't teach them a posture or breathing technique, or a particular mantra. He encouraged them, and us, to talk with God. He gave us his prayer, the Our Father. He wants us to talk to God together, because He said not, *My Father*, but *Our Father.* Words connect us with the supernatural.

Often we hear in church that we should listen for God's voice in our prayers or lives. There is a sense in which this is true, and a sense in which this is misleading. God has already spoken to us through the Bible, and so we can hear God's message to us, communicated through the people who wrote the Bible. It is essential to listen to (read, study, and pray about) this message. But, apart from the Bible, can we ever literally hear God speaking to us?

The Bible describes quite a few people hearing the voice of God in the Old Testament and New Testament. What's interesting to me is that none of them were listening for or expecting to hear God's voice. It was a total surprise to all of them. It was even a shock to some of them. The apostle Paul on the road to Damascus was not listening for the voice of God. It came as a surprise, and knocked him to the ground and blinded him. But God did speak to him. God speaks in His time, and in His way, clearly and specifically to some people, and not other people. But He has spoken richly and generally, through the creation and the

Bible, in the Incarnation of Jesus Christ and the uniqueness of the human being. These express God's Word, and the effect of His Word, and we should give careful attention to them. But to believe that God will speak a personal word to me, apart from the Bible, is a different matter.

Some people still expect it. They listen for God's voice about various concerns, such as whether to *buy a Ford,* or, *give money to the Pakistani mission,* or, *elect this elder and not that one.* It is possible God will speak personally to you in a prayer, but according to the Bible, *listening* for Him to speak doesn't seem to have a big effect on hearing Him. Rather, the Bible tells us that when He speaks, we hear, irrespective of whether we're listening for Him or not.

What does this mean practically? Let's say we are trying to decide whether to buy that car, that Ford we saw at the dealership, although our financial situation is tight. We know that God is a God of big things and of little things, and that everything matters to Him, and so we want to make sure that we use our money wisely. What should we do? Can we pray to God about this for guidance? Of course we can, and should. We could pray for wisdom. We could pray for sensitivity to circumstances to help us make a good decision. However, when we ask God to make the decision for us, very often *He says, No, you decide. You're a human being, not a puppet. I'm not deciding for you.* You decide. But it's still good that you bring the question to God, because we are taught in Philippians, *In everything, by prayer and supplication, bring your requests to God.* It doesn't say just bring the things He might be interested in. It says everything. That includes the Ford. But He's not going to dehumanize us by dictating to us all the details of our lives.

Sometimes miracles can happen in response to prayer. We may be sitting at the kitchen table, and suddenly we get a phone call from our friend in Oklahoma who says, *Hey, I've got this old Ford I don't need any more, do you know anybody who needs a car?* These things do happen, not all the time, but they happen. Nevertheless, you shouldn't wait for something like that to occur before you make a decision. You might end up waiting the rest of your life and never buy a car at all, when you might really need one.

In thinking about the supernatural, we need to remember that we are forbidden to control it. That's why magic is forbidden. Magic is the control of the supernatural. Some churches try to get around this prohibition in subtle ways. For instance, some churches believe and practice that, after the band has warmed up and the singing is loud enough, the Holy Spirit will arrive. This is magic. The idea seems to be that the Holy Spirit will show up at 8:00, but not at 7:00, because the band is still warming up. It's only when we do our thing that the Holy Spirit will show up. This is not a good practice.

A Comprehensive Spirituality

Spirituality is not a part of our lives, but all of our lives. A comprehensive spirituality includes all the triangles we have considered: creativity, rationality, morality, emotions, language, relationships, body, and the supernatural.

Everything we do, except sin, is part of our spirituality. We should not see our lives as divided into the spiritual or supernatural versus the natural parts but integrated as a whole.

We don't understand all of this perfectly or see it all clearly. God has promised those who believe in Jesus that we will be completely restored to His intention for us. "Now we see as through a glass darkly, then we will see face to face. Now I know in part, then I shall know fully, even as I am fully known." (I Corinthians 13:12).

Smoked Glass

Purely beginning
Burning through various deaths
Our hearts turn to ice

Falsely beginning
Purified by Spirit's fire
Our hearts melt to flesh.

- a pair of Haiku by the author

32 Questions

1. *What is hell?*

Hell is part of the supernatural. God does not want death. God wants us to live. It's not God's will that any sinner should die, but that all will turn to Him, and live. In God's reality there is life, but not death. Death is a result of trying to live in another reality. So, although death actually happens, it isn't real. How does hell fit into this?

It seems to me that if we choose to consistently live outside of reality, the most likely thing that will happen is that we *unbecome.* The person in the Bible who spoke most about hell was Jesus. His word for hell was Gehenna. Gehenna was a real place. It was the garbage dump in the Kidron Valley, outside of Jerusalem. Gehenna was a good image because the garbage was burned, and the fire burned twenty-four hours a day. The flame didn't go out. The question, in terms of hell, is *What happens to the garbage?* We know the flame is eternal, but does the garbage burn eternally, or is the garbage burned up? Part of Jesus's message is that if we consider ourselves garbage, we will be garbage, and will go into the fire.

2. *Another question is, Where does the fire come from?*

It seems to me that it must come from God. Some people have a vague idea that the devil makes the fire, but I don't think the devil makes anything. The devil is not a creator. The devil is an accuser. The devil lives in unreality, in rebellion against God. He invites and entices other creatures to come and be with him, which is his way of consuming them. But the fire that we read about in the Bible comes from God. It is His glory. It is an eternal part of Him. The key issue, for us, is whether we encounter this fire as a *refining* fire versus a *consuming* fire. If we turn to God, and choose to live in His reality—if we want to be changed by Him—then we face the fire. It burns us and refines us, as silver being smelted in the crucible, as talked about in Malachai. The fire burns, and the impurities rise to the surface and are scraped off. The silver gets purer and purer; and the refiner is Jesus. He hovers over the boiling pot, and as the scum is scraped away, Jesus sees Himself in the silver, because we become more like Him as we are refined. However, if we don't turn to God, if we turn *away* from God, then the fire burns us from the back. The fire doesn't refine those who want to live in their own imagination, in their pride and vanity; it's the same fire, but it burns, consumes, and destroys. We know that the fire is eternal, because it's God, but again, the question is, is the garbage eternally burned or is the garbage burned up? It's a difficult question.

3. *A related question is, Is hell eternally self-perpetuating, or would God have to sustain it forever?*

Some people believe that God would, in fact, sustain such a parallel universe for eternity. It is a parallel universe, separate and apart, because it cannot exist within God's universe, which is truth and light, Spirit and love. This parallel universe is a false reality—proud, self-centered, destructive, and rebellious. Some would argue that God would not sustain such a separate universe, would not lend His creative power to keeping such a place in existence. In this case, since nothing can continue to exist without God's sustaining power, hell could not go on forever, but instead would fade away as those within it are burned up.

4. *We sometimes hear that the left part of the brain is more sequential and linear in its processing, and the right part of the brain is more wholistic in its processing. Does the structure of the brain have any correspondence to time and eternity?*

Probably not. The Bible tells us that we should have the mind of Christ, not the brain of Christ. The brain is a tool that the mind uses for thinking.

5. *What is the mind?*

We don't know entirely, but a passage that helps us understand the mind is from the Sermon on the Mount, where Jesus speaks of the eye being the lamp of the body. Jesus tells us when the eye is single, the body is full of light, but if the eye is evil, the body is full of darkness. When the eye is single, it sees everything in one focus and is undivided. The brain sees reality divided into linear and wholistic, but the mind is not divided unless it is evil.

6. *How do we come to this singleness of mind?*

By trusting God to do it for us. Trust corresponds to faith. I have faith that God will do to me and with me what is good and necessary. I make myself available to God working in me by trusting and obeying Him, so I am not totally passive. I choose to believe in God, I choose to trust Him, I choose to walk in the way that the Spirit indicates I should walk.

7. *What should people do when this walk leads to pain and suffering?*

We should accept the pain and suffering as growing pains. The last beatitude in the Sermon on the Mount is *Blessed are those who are persecuted for the sake of Jesus, for theirs is the kingdom of heaven.* When we follow Jesus, we are in two kingdoms, the kingdom of this world and the kingdom of heaven. There is a struggle and a battle. The stress and suffering of this battle are signs of life and membership in the kingdom of God.

8. *Why do you think so many people associate being more spiritual with having transcendent or supernatural experiences?*

One reason is that is seems to make spirituality easier. It is a kind of escape from full reality. People suffer in the natural world, and want the supernatural to be more real than the natural. People expect not to suffer in the supernatural part of reality. We are motivated to think this way by the devil, who wants to get us to see reality partly and not fully. Seeing reality fully means seeing it as both natural and supernatural.

9. *If we see a vision, or have some other supernatural experience, that just comes to us, can we trust it?*

We need to test our supernatural experiences and see if they belong to the Biblical truth as a whole. In I John 4:1-3, we are told to test our experiences to see if they acknowledge that Jesus Christ has come in the flesh. This means that the supernatural has become natural; the eternal has entered into time. Any vision or experience should not lead us away from this truth.

There's a story about Charles Spurgeon, a Baptist pastor in London. He was walking down the aisle of his church to preach in the pulpit. An angel of light stood in his way and said, "Charles Spurgeon, I have a message from the Lord for you." Spurgeon said, "I'm busy now, I'm about to preach." The angel said, "This is a very urgent message." Spurgeon said, "Okay, tell me." The angel said, "Your name is written in the Lamb's Book of Life." Spurgeon said, "The Bible has already told me that, and you are tempting me to believe the word of an angel. Go away." This is an example of testing the spirits. We are all different, and should not try to copy each other, but have the attitude of requiring clarity from a supernatural experience. The basic question, in various forms, is *Has Jesus Christ come in the flesh?* Spurgeon did not ask this question literally, but his concern was for Jesus Christ who is the Word of God, incarnated and written, to be the basis of his life.

10. Are there people who are more prone to an awareness of the supernatural? If so, what guidance would you give these people?

Some people, especially children, seem to be more aware of the supernatural than other people. My advice would be not to reject this awareness, but to be careful. If we emphasize the supernatural too much, we can come to believe that the supernatural is more real than the natural, which is not true. The belief that the supernatural is more real comes principally from the devil, but also through some philosophers like Plato. Christ-ism is not mysticism. Jesus is not only supernaturally real, but naturally real. The Word became flesh without becoming unspiritual.

11. Silence and stillness are often emphasized in non-Christian spiritual systems, especially meditative systems. Should silence and stillness play a role in the Christian life?

Yes, we should give space for listening to God, who speaks through his word, the Bible, and in other ways. We should be careful not to confuse silence and stillness with prayer, which is committed language.

12. If spiritual equals totally real, does spiritual also equal humility?

I wouldn't say that spiritual equals humility, but that humility is spiritual. Humility is basically realism, accepting who God is, what He does, and want He wants. When God called Moses at the burning bush to lead Israel, Moses said, *No, I am not qualified.* This was pride. Then, Moses accepted that God's will was right, which was humility. Moses was called the most humble man alive. He had the power of life and death over a million people, and he was humble.

13. What are the words the Bible uses to talk about spirituality?

When the Bible speaks of spirituality, it begins with God. It even says "God is Spirit". The words the Bible uses for spirit are ruah and pneuma, Hebrew and Greek words that both mean "wind". When the Bible says the Spirit blows where it wills, it says "The wind winds". The Spirit is expression or what goes out. A person has a spirit. So does a book or a song or a political party or a family or a church. They all express themselves and are active. The spirit expresses the whole person. It involves every part of the person. The fact of Jesus being the word of God through which everything was made shows us the creative effect of this wind or expression.

In the Gospel of John, 4:24, Jesus says "God is spirit". He doesn't say that God is spiritual or has spiritual parts. God is all spirit, so our understanding of what is spiritual is going to need to include all that we find out about God. Notice also that it doesn't work to say *Spirit is God.* If we think that way, then we end up starting with our experience of what we think spirit is and what we feel spirit is. We end up saying God is my understanding of spirit. It doesn't work because it begins with us. The same is true of love. If we want to know what love is, then we need to find out what is God-like. God is *love* is the correct equation. The false equation is love is God. Many people in our day, in post-modern times, believe in the false equation. They say My experience of love, or my assumptions or aspirations about love, are God. *If I know about these things then I'll know about God.* But I won't. I'll just know something about my insanity, about my own distortions. But if we say it the other way around—God is love—then we begin with God and can find out what love actually is. We need to let God define love in terms of Himself. The same is true of spirit. Everything we find out about God *is* spiritual, including the Incarnation.

14. Is technology spiritually evil?

New technologies in our world are starting to allow us to manipulate basic aspects of our being, whether through gene editing, creating interfaces between the brain and artificial intelligence, or other means. Should we be pursuing this? There should probably be some limits on these activities, although it may depend on how and why the technology is being used. Generally speaking, these technologies would be considered problematic and indeed evil if they were to, for instance, reduce or diminish basic aspects of our spirituality, reduce our ability to make choices, or reduce our ability to experience guilt and to see our need for forgiveness. So there should probably be limits, although we need to think and pray carefully to get an idea of the best way forward.

15. *What were the consequences of the fall?*

Death. By "death", I mean alienation and separation of things
that God intends to be together. By "things" I mean, for example,
one person and another person, people and God, and people
from themselves, so that a person's body is separated from
their mind and their spirit while alive to an extent, and then
experiences a permanent separation when the body disintegrates.
There is also an alienation of the human part of creation (human
beings) from the non-human part of creation (plants, animals,
rocks, streams, etc.). Death is unspiritual. Comprehensive
spirituality, which is a gift of God through Jesus Christ, destroys
death, and restores all of the relationship that God intends.

16. *How can we live as fully human as possible in a fallen world?*

Actively and passively. We allow God to live in us, and work in us
for life, and we make choices to follow His guidance in His word
(the Bible) and from the Holy Spirit who lives in us. All of the
triangles need to be included in the choices that we make, so that
we have a wholistic life and spirituality.

17. *What is the difference between moral and ethical?*

Moral means living within the absolute life guidelines of God.
Immoral means living outside of those guidelines. Ethical means
living within the temporary life guidelines of a culture. Unethical
means living outside of those guidelines. People draw ethical
lines. God draws moral lines.
If you have sex with someone who is not your spouse, you have
crossed the line. But if you *think* about sex with someone who is
not your spouse, you have also crossed the line.
We never are in the situation where we have not crossed the line.
We are always sinners. We always need God's grace. We cannot
keep ourselves safe.

18. *Do scientists cross moral lines?*

Scientists have always crossed the line into immorality. Ancient agronomical scientists discovered methods of intensive crop production, and destroyed the soil in the Tigris-Euphrates valley around 3000 or 4000 BC. Scientists have always taken what they discover out of the whole context of God's creation and been destructive. God wants people to explore His creation scientifically, but He wants us to take good care of creation with what we learn, and not just to impose a limited, egotistical manipulation on it that destroys it. So, when we begin to think about nano technology and things like that, the question remains the same as it was in ancient history. Science is mandated by God but it must be used responsibly and carefully in the whole context of God's creation, so that we don't reduce His creation and destroy it.

19. *How can we tell if our church has become too rational in its interpretation of Scripture?*

Even a little bit of rationality is wrong, if it is decontextualized from love. So if we think we can contain a vital and lively understanding in our minds, without living it out in love, we make a big mistake. Rationality is good and right, but it has to function within the context of love. If it becomes independent from love, it produces death. So the question is not *if* there is too much or too little rationality, but is the rationality practiced in the context of love?

There could be a church in a university town that has such a high level of rationality that the average person would feel alienated, but the rationality is practiced in the context of love, so there is no problem with it. On the other hand, there could be a church in a rural farming community, where nobody has ever been to college, and the rationality is practiced in a legalistic, egotistical, and exclusionary way; in this case, the rationality would be destructive.

20. *Is it spiritual to take psychedelic substances to alleviate a psychiatric or medical condition?*

I would think so, generally.

21. *Is it spiritual to take psychedelic substances to come into contact with supernatural beings or realms?*

We are required to test the spirits to see if they are from God. The test, as I mentioned earlier, is *Has Jesus Christ come in the flesh?* So, if a psychedelic drug gives us an experience that teaches us that the supernatural is more real than the natural, it is wrong (because Jesus Christ has come in the flesh and remained fully spiritual).

22. *Can you give an example of the shalom of God in the context of suffering?*

Shalom is well-being and security in God's truth and love. Shalom is a foundation and a framework for life that God provides. That foundation is equally effective whether we are happy or sad, or safe or in danger. It is not an absence of conflict, but a security within the conflict. The shalom of God is larger than the conflicts that we experience.

When I was hospitalized for depression, I was very, very sick, and in terrible pain. When I asked myself, "Am I safe in God's love?", the answer was always, "Oh yes, of course!"

23. *Were there ever moments when you lost touch with this shalom?*

There are moments when we all lose touch with it. It's a fallen world; we are all sinners. But in moments when we lose touch with God's shalom can be very happy or triumphant moments. When we are happy or triumphant, we can be tempted to become self-centered and to know good and evil in terms of our own experience and imagination, rather than in terms of God's truth. So I would say the happy, comfortable, and achieving moments of life are more dangerous than the moments of life that we do not enjoy. When we suffer, we tend to become more aware of our need of God. When we are triumphant or happy or comfortable, we tend to forget our need of God. To forget our need of God is to lose shalom. This corresponds to the first beatitude—blessed are the poor in spirit, for theirs is the kingdom of heaven—because it is only when we know that we need God that we have shalom.

24. *How can we become more committed in our use of language?*

Write down questions and statements, and come back to them after a day or two, and see if you would sign your name to them. Re-write until the questions and statements stabilize, and are the same every day. Some of my students have tried this, and it works. Others found it too hard and gave up. This exercise can be humiliating, because we may realize that we are chaotic and not committed to our speech. Although we can see that it would be possible to become more committed to our speech, the world around us encourages us in chaos. The people around us might say "Chill", "Loosen up", "Don't worry about it", "Just go with the flow", or "Whatever". Somebody once told me, "Don't become a wordsmith". To become more committed in the use of language is to be counter-cultural and anti-social in our present post-modern culture—and in this way, to become more spiritual.

25. *Where does the human yearning for discovery and pattern-breaking come from?*

God. God wanted to make creatures in His image. Human beings are in His image. The other creatures (animals) are not. Human beings are commanded by God to continue His process of creation by increasing the complexity of creation.
For instance, God made sheep and goats to wander in nature and follow the seasons. Human beings increase the complexity of sheep and goats by housing them in permanent and stable situations. What God does is called creation, and what people do is called art, because it's artificial.

26. *What do people mean today when they say they are spiritual but not religious?*

Largely, I don't know. So, if someone says that to me, I will ask them what they mean. Assuming that we know what another person means is often a great handicap to communication.

27. *You said eternity is permanent and time is temporary. If time is temporary, then is it a distortion?*

The creation as God made it was perfect. The relationship of time to eternity was perfect, without distortion. But sin and rebellion produced an alienation in reality that needs to be overcome by Jesus. The creation in time is an expression of the reality in eternity. God lives in eternity, before and outside the creation. Time and eternity are matrices of sequence. In space, things happen in time. Outside of space, things happen in eternity. There are various interfaces between time and eternity, the most important being revelation and prayer. When Jesus appears, everything will be brought together, into one matrix, and we will live in eternity.

28. *How can we feel the working of the Holy Ghost?*

We are filled with the Holy Spirit when we believe in Jesus.
There is nothing in the Bible about how the Holy Spirit feels.
At the same time, there is nothing in the Bible that tells us that
the Holy Spirit doesn't feel like anything. But it doesn't tell us
what we feel or how we feel.

29. *What is a blessing?*

A blessing is an enlargement of life—whereas a curse is a
shrinking of life. We have generally a serious misconception that
blessing feels good. Many blessings feel bad. The clearest example
is the dentist. The dentist is a blessing. He feels bad. We're afraid
of him. We avoid him. I think that's a symbol of all of life. The
blessings very often feel bad, and the curses feel good. If you fall
and break your leg on the street, and you're lying there in pain,
and a doctor comes to you and says, "Oh, you poor dear, you must
be in terrible pain, I see the bone sticking out of your skin, I will
bless you"—and he injects you with morphine. In three seconds
you feel wonderful. Then he says, "Now you are blessed," and he
walks away. Are you blessed? No, you are cursed. Life is really
confusing, and we need to look into the Bible and see what is
blessing and what is cursing and to walk by faith.

30. *What is heaven?*

Heaven is the supernatural dimensions of reality. The dimensions
of heaven are similar to, but different from, the dimensions of
the natural reality. For instance, the natural reality functions
basically in time, and the supernatural reality functions basically
in eternity. Both time and eternity are matrices of sequence,
which connect with each other. This means that every point of
time is present to every point of eternity. At the end of temporal
history, the prayer that Jesus taught us to pray, "Your kingdom

come, Your will be done, on earth as it is in heaven", will be fully answered. The hope of Christianity is not that we will go to heaven, but that heaven will come to us. Time and eternity will conflate, and be one matrix of sequence. The separation between heaven and earth will end.

31. Sometimes people ask, "What will it be like to be in heaven?" Do you have any thoughts about this?

There are two stages or phases. One is to be with God after we die, but before the resurrection of the dead and the coming of heaven to earth. This is an in-between stage. The Bible indicates that people who die in the Lord will be with him, and know that they are with him, and also longing for their new resurrection bodies. The final reality is when heaven comes to earth, and heaven and earth are united, and we have our resurrection bodies. We have an example of a resurrection body in the resurrection of Jesus Christ. He ate and drank, and talked with people, and moved instantly through space and appeared physically in rooms without coming through the door or the window. So, the resurrection body will be similar to our natural body, and recognizable, but also different in ways that we do not fully know yet.

32. Why would we need a resurrection body that can eat and drink, since eating and drinking are associated with needing to give a physical body energy and to keep it alive?

It doesn't make any sense in terms of time and physical dimensions, but we will be in other dimensions, so it will make sense. However, we cannot understand this yet, from our current point of view. So the answer to the question is, *Wait and see.*